Let the Sea Take It

Brittani Hirsch

BookLeaf Publishing

India | USA | UK

Presentation by *BookLeaf Publishing*

Web: www.bookleafpub.com

E-mail: info@bookleafpub.com

ISBN: 9789358317213

First edition 2024

DEDICATION

To love- a powerful and beautiful thing that's hard to find and even harder to hold onto

Moving On

Strength is watching a love letter
Crinkle and curl at the edges as
Flames lick the words off the page
Like love never even existed at all

And So I Begin Again

Well, listen good. Because
I'm proof
Light lives beyond the dark.
A life told with seasons
With shattered hearts
With broken promises.
This story changes. And changes.
And changes.
For the better.

Wrecked

I'm trying hard not to hate you
For letting your demons destroy
The lifetime of love you promised
Me.

I'm trying hard not to hate you
For letting me believe that you
Were someone beautiful when
Behind your real mask lurks a
Monster.

I'm trying hard not to hate you
For tightening the noose around
my neck and bringing my blood to a
Boil.

I'm trying hard not to hate you
For wrecking our dreams and
Building your own future with
Her.

Most of all, I hate that I can't hate you
Even though you brought me down
To the darkest hours I've ever
Known.

Nature's Tantrum

Thunderstorms are beautiful
when the skies thrash,
bruised in violet verde hues,
and electricity pulses through the air
electrocuting with a rage so deep
that the night begins to scream

it's a reminder that, sometimes,
even the Heavens need to let it all out

Rescued

5

When the sun falls asleep she snuggles into me
So deep that her whiskers become tangled in
My dreams and our hearts whisper melodies to
each other

Morning light manifests a maniacal monster
Trying to shake loose the energies bottled up
Barking and biting at the air, as if it's responsible
for awakening her beast

Angel by night, demon by day
Either way, she saved me.

Betrayal

The pain will come
And when it does
Bleed it out
Spill it out
Cry it out
So it doesn't shut out
What's truly meant
For you

Sandcastle

all that time spent
arranging
grains of sand into
a fragile kingdom
only to be
caved in by one
gurgling breath

And so
build and rebuild
each turret stronger
each moat longer
each wave conquered

and when the time comes
for the sea to take it away
let it go

Helpless

Like a house of cards
I crumble under the slightest gasp
Disconnected from the
Stability
Comfort
Diamonds
Falling to the ground
Kindling ready to burn
And only hands not yours
Can rebuild me

Deception

You promised me a lifetime
Instead you left me
with

Eight months of lies and betrayal
Seven years of thinking it was always my fault
Six coastline vacations ending in arguments
Five days late alone in the bathroom
Four pointless sessions with a professional
Three people in one marriage
Two many questions unanswered
One blessing lost

And zero ounces of trust.

Oatmeal

The day after I found out
My mom tried to get me to eat
She made me oatmeal
My tears cascaded
into the bowl
I took one bite
It didn't taste the same
I used to love oatmeal
But now I never will.

The Call

One after another the call comes in and again
From an unrecognized number
The December sun plays peek-a-boo
like it's afraid to witness what's to come
And then I speak after a dozen rings
My world shatters
Time stands still
Like all the world's clock batteries have died
And at the exact same moment and
A cry so piercing rips from my chest
that it tears the day in half
And I'm gasping for air that is
smeared the color of a spliced heart

Evolution of a Broken Heart

When peace shatters into darkness
And darkness stirs up rage
And rage transforms to revenge
And revenge merges with guilt
And guilt splays open hurt
And hurt is masked by apologies
And apologies coil into second chances
And second chances mirror no change
And change settles as the new norm
And the new norm molds courage
And courage blossoms into strength
And strength morphs in a smile
And a smile emerges from happiness
And happiness recasts the future
And the future grows into what I deserve.

Dusty Memories

If you're wondering where I still see you
It's sitting in a booth at our favorite restaurant
It's watching Sunday football in sweatpants
It's mixing a Bloody Mary with extra green
olives

If you're wondering where I still see you
It's driving with the windows down and country
blasting
It's walking the dogs after the sun dips below the
horizon
It's pulling the thorniest weeds in the backyard

If you're wondering where I still see you
It's dancing Two Step in the living room at
midnight
It's grinning childishly at the magic of a Disney
commercial
It's grilling burgers on the deck in the middle of
July

If you're wondering where I still see you
It's in the black and white memories I keep
tucked
Far

Far
Far
in the back shelf of my last life
A place where I don't let myself wander to
anymore.

Dog-Earred

I will always remember
How you folded me at my corner
Like you were desperate to come back
And finish our story

Static

I wish I lived the way I wrote
Passionately
Obsessively
Unapologetically
Without fear of being judged

I'd live by taking the leap with a stranger
Spiraling into the maddening depths
of distant lands and endless dreams
I'd drown myself in the vast ocean of love
Instead of living like a television
Turned to a dead station
Afraid of color

Fierce

Remember what you must do
when they keep you waiting
keep you wondering
keep you guessing your worth
when they mistake
your silence for weakness
and take advantage of
your heart

You awaken
every monster
every lion
every beast
and you remind them
what hell looks like
behind the mask of
of a gentle soul.

Next Chapter

I know this door
It doesn't need a key
When I step through it
Dreams comfort me

Stones line its path
Stretching for the door
The next chapter awaits me
Promising so much more

The threshold beckons to me
Tall and inviting in its frame
Confident that as I step through
My bitterness will be tamed

The breath in my soul
Courses through my veins
This life may have shattered
But hope for the next still remains.

Darkness

When I was little
the dark was a
haunting place to be
monsters loomed and
nightmares thrived
and floor creaks
meant you weren't alone

Stupid me
Grew up thinking
I could trust you
And instead you reinforced
how the night
hides the truth
casts false silhouettes
pockets reality

and that's why
I'm still scared
of being left in the dark

Abandoned

Sometimes
despite the hype
stories must be
abandoned
endings hanging loose
unlike how
you imagined them
leaving questions
lingering within
chapters dangling
in the abyss
forever unread

Rock Bottom

That moment when you wake up
And in a split second
Reality catches you up to speed
Fuzzily coming into frame
Reminding you that you'd
Rather close your eyes
Live with the lights out
Fall asleep forever

To The One

look for me at the edge of the sea
where the tides fall in love with the shore
and the unexpected washes up at your feet
promise me you'll give me more
than expectations, betrayal, and silence
that you'll quench my thirst for a life
that ends my desperate hunger for love

www.ingramcontent.com/pod-product-compliance
Lightning Source LLC
La Vergne TN
LVHW050301200726
843509LV00015B/3101